SCIENCE ACADEMY

PERFECT PULL

BY KIRSTY HOLMES

CRABTREE
PUBLISHING COMPANY
WWW.CRABTREEBOOKS.COM

CRABTREE
PUBLISHING COMPANY
WWW.CRABTREEBOOKS.COM

Author:
Kirsty Holmes

Editorial director:
Kathy Middleton

Editors:
Madeline Tyler, Janine Deschenes

Proofreader:
Petrice Custance

Graphic design:
Ian McMullen

Prepress technician:
Katherine Berti

Print coordinator:
Katherine Berti

Library and Archives Canada Cataloguing in Publication

Title: Perfect pull / by Kirsty Holmes.
Names: Holmes, Kirsty, author.
Description: Series statement: Science academy | Originally
published: King's Lynn: BookLife, 2020. | Includes index.
Identifiers: Canadiana (print) 2020357727 |
Canadiana (ebook) 2020357735 |
ISBN 9781427130556 (hardcover) |
ISBN 9781427130594 (softcover) |
ISBN 9781427130631 (HTML)
Subjects: LCSH: Force and energy—Juvenile literature. |
LCSH: Motion—Juvenile literature.
Classification: LCC QC73.4 .H65 2021 | DDC j531/.6—dc23

Library of Congress Cataloging-in-Publication Data

Names: Holmes, Kirsty, author.
Title: Perfect pull / by Kirsty Holmes.
Description: New York : Crabtree Publishing Company, 2021. | Series:
Science academy | Includes index. | Audience: Ages 6–9 | Audience:
Grades 2–3 | Summary: "It's Sports Week at Science Academy! Every year
the other school wins the tug-of-war competition. But Katie is
determined to win. Join Katie as she tries to learn everything there is
to know about pulling forces to knock her opponent off balance. Simple
sentences and easy-to-understand examples make learning about forces
understandable and fun"— Provided by publisher.
Identifiers: LCCN 2020045836 (print) |
LCCN 2020045837 (ebook) |
ISBN 9781427130556 (hardcover) |
ISBN 9781427130594 (paperback) |
ISBN 9781427130631 (ebook)
Subjects: LCSH: Force and energy—Juvenile literature.
Classification: LCC QC73.4 .H655 2021 (print) |
LCC QC73.4 (ebook) | DDC 531/.6—dc23
LC record available at https://lccn.loc.gov/2020045836
LC ebook record available at https://lccn.loc.gov/2020045837

All images are courtesy of Shutterstock.com, unless otherwise specified.
With thanks to Getty Images, Thinkstock Photo, and iStockphoto.

Front Cover: LightField Studios, ivector, Sonic_S , Pixfiction, Africa Studio,
Alexapicso, Somchai Som, ffolas, Tapui, VectorPot, Ohn Mar.

Interior: Background – TheBestGraphics, Arrows – Sasha Ka. Characters:
Lewis – Cookie Studio. Dee Dee – LightField Studios. Kush: Gratsias Adhi
Hernawan. Ling: GOLFX. Paige: Oleksandr Zamuruiev. Katie: LightField
Studios. BudE – sdecoret. Professor Adams – HBRH. 511. Monkey Business
Images, maxim ibragimov, Jacob Lund. 13 – italianestro, Erik Gonzalez,
alexei_tm, Joshua Sanderson Media. 12-13 – Zurijeta. 13 – Roblan. 2–21 –
4 PM production, gzaleckas, Billion Photos, Wojciech Wrzesien, altanaka.
23 – Ljupco Smokovski, unguryanu, Krasowit, yalayana

All facts, statistics, web addresses, and URLs in this book were verified as valid
and accurate at time of writing. No responsibility for any changes to external
websites or references can be accepted by either the author or publisher.

Crabtree Publishing Company
www.crabtreebooks.com   1-800-387-7650

Published by Crabtree Publishing Company in 2021
© 2020 BookLife Publishing Ltd.

Published in Canada
Crabtree Publishing
616 Welland Ave.
St. Catharines, Ontario
L2M 5V6

Published in the United States
Crabtree Publishing
347 Fifth Ave
Suite 1402-145
New York, NY 10016

Printed in the U.S.A./122020/CG20201014

CONTENTS

Page 4   Attendance

Page 6   Morning Lesson

Page 8   Lunchtime

Page 10   Afternoon Lesson

Page 12   Solve It with Science!

Page 14   Balanced or Unbalanced?

Page 16   Katie Pulls It Together

Page 18   Heave Ho!

Page 20   All Kinds of Pulling Forces

Page 22   Problem Solved

Page 23   Homework

Page 24   Glossary and Index

ATTENDANCE

Another day at Science Academy has begun.
Time to take attendance! Meet class 201.

Lewis

Favorite subject:
Electricity

Ling

Favorite subject:
Pushing forces

Dee Dee

Favorite subject:
Movement

Paige

Favorite subject:
Magnets

Katie

Favorite subject:
Pulling forces

Ravi

Favorite subject:
Energy

Today's lessons are all about forces called pulls.
The students will learn answers to these questions:

- What is a force?
- What is a pull?
- What are balanced and unbalanced forces?
- How can we use pulling forces?

Bud-E
Favorite subject:
Being helpful!

Science Academy is a school
especially for kids who love
science and solving problems!
Do I hear the bell?

MORNING LESSON

It's Sports Week at Science Academy. Professor Adams explains that each student will **compete** in a different **event**. Their challenge is to use science ideas to help them succeed. Professor Adams reads the list of events to the class.

Lewis, you're doing the math marathon. Ling, you will compete in the robot sack race. Does everyone know what to do?

This year, Katie will compete in the tug-of-war event. She has tough competition. Emily is also competing. She won the event last year. In the tug-of-war event, each person pulls on a rope. He or she tries to pull the opposite person over a line between them.

How can science help Katie win the event?

LUNCHTIME

All morning, the students study science ideas that will help them succeed in their event. At lunchtime, Bud-E helps the students train for their events outside.

Drop and give me 20 push-ups! Go, go, go!

Katie isn't training with the others. She decides to spend lunchtime looking at books about forces. In the morning, she learned that a force is a push or pull that makes something move.

I need to learn all I can about pulling forces. Emily will be hard to beat.

AFTERNOON LESSON

Bud-E asks Katie why she is reading a book instead of training with the other students. Katie tells Bud-E that she has more to learn about forces. She shows her books to Bud-E.

Bud-E, can you teach me anything about forces?

Bud-E explains that you can't see forces, but you can see the **effect** they have on the things around us. Different forces can move objects in different ways.

A push is a force that moves something away from you.

A pull is a force that moves something closer to you.

Gravity is a force that pulls things down to the ground.

Objects can move in straight lines, circles, and back-and-forth.

SOLVE IT WITH SCIENCE!

Katie needs to use a pulling force to win the tug-of-war event. She needs to move Emily closer to her and across the line. She will use her hands to **apply** the pulling force on the rope.

Can you think of other ways people use pulling forces?

We use pulling forces every day. Pulling forces make things move. They can make things speed up, slow down, and change direction.

A tow truck pulls a broken car to make it move.

Lifting a glass is a pulling force. You bring the glass closer to you.

You pull on the apple to pick it from the tree.

You pull on a dog's leash to make it change direction.

BALANCED OR UNBALANCED?

When you fly a kite, you pull on the string to hold the kite in place and move it across the sky. At the same time, the wind is pushing the kite away from you. Two **opposite** forces—a pull and a push—are affecting the kite at the same time.

To keep the kite in the sky, the wind's pushing force and your pulling force on the string need to be balanced. This means they are the same size.

When opposite forces affecting one object are balanced, the object does not move. To make the object move, one force needs to be stronger than the other. Forces that have different strengths are unbalanced.

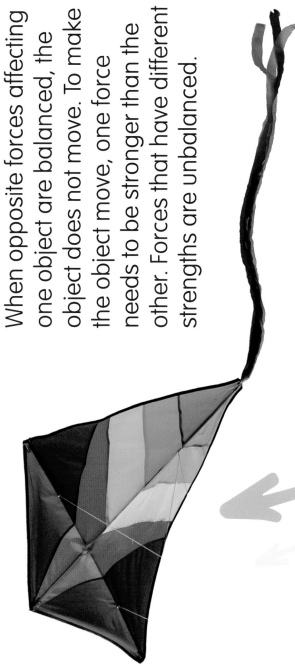

If you pull hard on the string, the kite will come down. But if the pushing force of the wind is stronger than your pulling force, the kite could fly away!

KATIE PULLS IT TOGETHER

Katie learned that balanced and unbalanced forces will be at work during the tug-of-war event. There will be two opposite pulling forces on the rope.

Katie will pull on the rope in one direction. Emily will pull on the rope in the other direction.

If Katie and Emily's pulling forces are balanced, neither girl will move. To win the tug-of-war event, Katie's pulling force must be stronger than Emily's.

The pulling forces on the rope need to be unbalanced. If Katie's pulling force is stronger than Emily's, she will move across the line.

HEAVE HO!

Finally, it is the day of the tug-of-war event. Katie and Emily stand face-to-face. Katie has learned a lot about forces. She knows that the pulling forces on the rope need to be unbalanced.

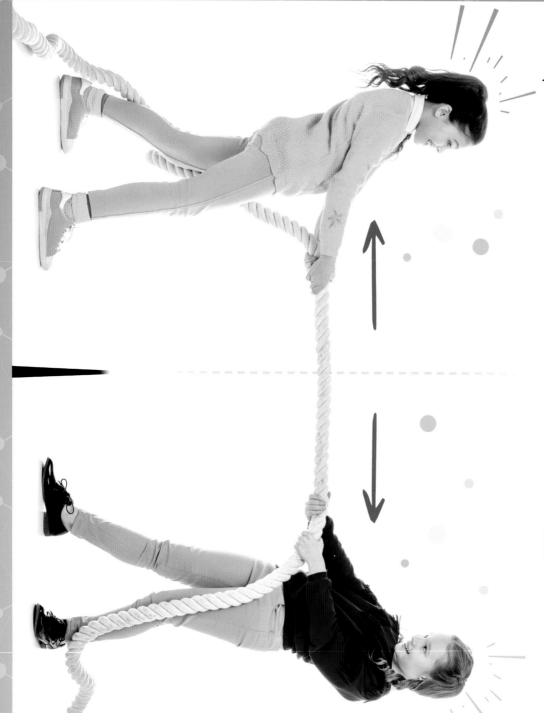

When Katie and Emily start the event, their pulling forces are balanced.

Katie pulls harder and harder. Slowly, Emily moves closer to the line. Then, Emily steps forward and crosses the line! Katie has won!

Katie used a stronger pulling force than Emily. She unbalanced the two forces.

ALL KINDS OF PULLING FORCES

People use many kinds of pulling forces. You can pull something up or down. You can use strong and light pulling forces. What ways do you use pulling forces?

When you jump in the air, gravity pulls you back to the ground.

You use a light pulling force to make a yo-yo move upward.

When you climb, you use a pulling force to move yourself up.

You pull a zipper down to close a backpack.

Lifting a dog can take a bigger pulling force.

PROBLEM SOLVED

Katie is the winner of the tug-of-war event. All of the Science Academy students did their best during Sports Week. With the help of science, they all win a medal!

HOMEWORK

Look around your home or school. How many things need a pulling force to move? Make a list. Here are some examples.

Backpack

Socks

Weights

Window blinds

GLOSSARY

APPLY To put on or use

COMPETE To take part in a contest or competition

EFFECT A change, result, or influence that happens due to a cause

EVENT A contest that is part of a sports competition

GRAVITY The force that pulls objects with mass, or weight, toward the ground

FORCE A push or pull that creates movement

OPPOSITE Being on the other side or completely different from something

INDEX

BALANCED FORCES 5, 14, 15, 16, 17, 18, 19

CLIMBING 21

GRAVITY 11, 20

LIFTING 13, 21

MOVEMENT 11, 12, 13, 17, 19, 23

OPPOSITE FORCES 14, 15, 16, 17

PUSH 4, 9, 11, 14, 15

UNBALANCED FORCES 5, 14, 15, 16, 17, 18, 19